ACPL ITEM
DISCARDED

3 1833 00781 8005

P9-BVG-588

HOLIDAY COLLECTION

MOLE and TROLL
Trim the Tree

by Tony Johnston

pictures by Wallace Tripp

G. P. Putnam's Sons New York

For G. and G. with love and kisses

Text copyright © 1974 by Tony Johnston
Illustrations copyright © 1974 by Wallace Tripp
All rights reserved. Published simultaneously in
Canada by Longman Canada Limited, Toronto.
SBN: GB-399-60909-1
SBN: TR-399-20418-0
Library of Congress Catalog Card Number: 73-82024
PRINTED IN THE UNITED STATES OF AMERICA
04208

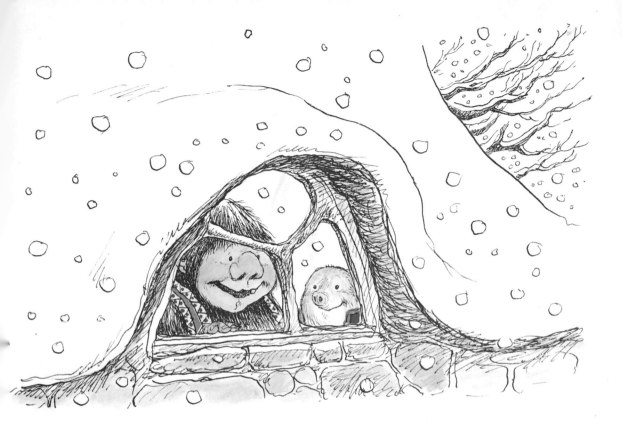

1820615

Christmas was coming. Soft snow
was drifting down on everything.
Mole and Troll were in a festive mood.
"Come on, Mole," said Troll.
"Let's go Christmas-treeing."
"I would love to," said Mole.

So they got bundled up. They put on big
snow coats. And snow scarfs. And
snow hats. And mittens. And ear muffs.
And snowshoes last of all. And off
they went.

Mole and Troll came to the pine forest.
Mole got very excited over all the
pretty trees.

"Let's see," he said. "I will take
that one and that one. No, wait!
I want those three and that little one
and *that* one, too!"

"Mole," said Troll.

"Yes, Troll?"

"You are just one mole, right?"

Mole looked at himself carefully.

"Right," he said.

"Then you only get one tree. Cover your eyes, and I will spin you around. The first tree you touch is yours."

"*Ours*, Troll. Let's share a tree this year."

"That is a fine idea!" said Troll.
So Mole covered his eyes. Troll spun
him around many times. Mole planned on
peeking through his fingers to make
a good choice. But he got too dizzy. He
wobbled smack into a little tree. It
was a fat sugar pine with fluffy
branches, a deep piny smell, and resin
dripping down the trunk.

"Perfect!" cried Troll. "Good
choice, Mole!"
"Thanks," said Mole, wobbling
around in a big circle.

Then Troll chopped the tree down with
a swish, swish, swish.
"I admire you, Troll," said Mole.
"Why?"
"You can chop down a moving tree so
easily."
"The tree is still," said Troll.
"*You* are moving. You are wobbling
all over."

"Oh," said Mole. And he toppled
over in the snow.

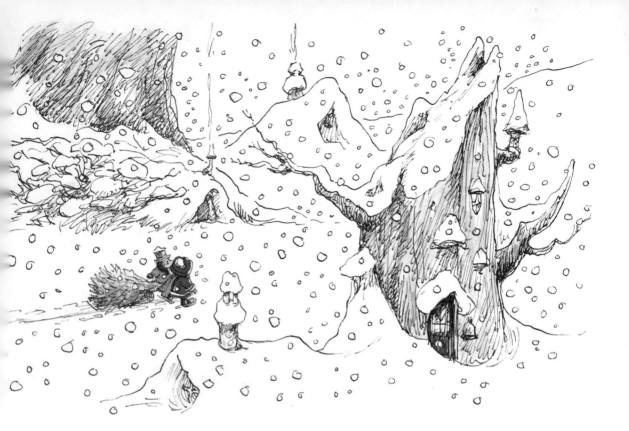

Troll dug Mole out. Then they loaded
the tree onto the toboggan. And they
went to Troll's house.

That afternoon the snow came down
thicker. It drifted up against the
houses. It piled up on the roofs. It
covered the trees and bushes in lovely
white.

Mole and Troll felt very jolly.

"Oh, Troll, let's trim our tree,"
said Mole.

And so they did.
Mole brought his ornaments in big
boxes. Troll took his ornaments down
from the shelf. And they began to trim
the tree.
Troll unwrapped a string of gay
colored lights.

"I always have gay colored
lights," he said as he put them on
the tree.
"I always have tiny twinkling
lights," said Mole. He put his
lights up, too.
Troll did not like that.
"Colored lights are better," he
said.
Mole sniffed.

Troll wound a sheet for snow around
the bottom of the tree. Mole did not
like that a bit.
"I always have cotton for snow,"
he said. "Cotton is better."
Troll sniffed.

Mole sat for a while on a little rug
stringing cranberries and popcorn.
Then he wound them all around the tree.
"What is *that?*" asked Troll.
"Popcorn and cranberries," said Mole.
"I always have them on my tree."
"That looks corny," grumbled Troll.
Mole sniffed loudly.

Then Troll put big globs of tinsel
all over the tree.
"There," he said. "That looks
shiny and nice."
"That looks crummy," said Mole.
"Besides, *good* tinsel goes on one
by one—not in *globs*."
Mole and Troll were getting mad. They
trimmed the tree silently with all of
their favorite things.
At last Mole climbed to the top of
the tree and put up a golden angel. Troll
could not stand that. He took it down
and put up a star.
Mole snatched it down and put the
angel back.
"I always have a star on top of my
tree!" said Troll loudly. "Take
that angel down!"

"I won't!" yelled Mole. "I always
have an angel on top!"
"A star!" shouted Troll.
"Angel!"
"Star!"
"Angel! Angel! Angel!"
"You are spoiling the tree with
junk!" cried Troll.

He grabbed at the angel to take it down.
But instead, the whole tree came
tumbling down on top of them.
Cranberries scattered everywhere.
Popcorn fell like rain.

Mole was *fuming* mad. He picked up a
cranberry and—*zip*. It hit Troll on
the ear. *Blip*—another cranberry hit
Troll on the end of his nose. *Plip,
plip, plip*. Another and another
and another hit Troll.
Troll leaped up in fury. He chased Mole
around and around the fallen tree.
"Just wait till I get you!" cried
Troll. "I will wrap you up in
lights and make you twinkle like a
little star!"

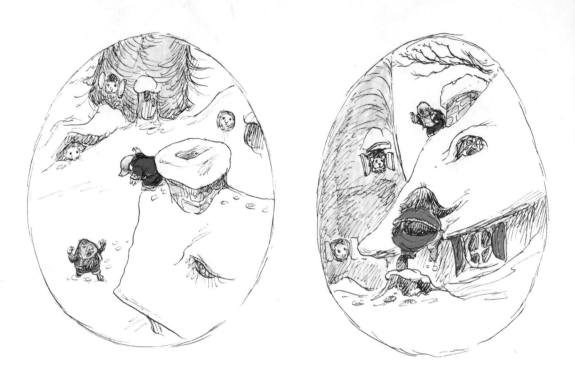

Mole puffed out the door, scrambled
onto the roof, and raced around the
chimney, throwing cranberries at
Troll and shouting, "No, you won't!
Leave me alone, you fuzzy, wuzzy troll!"
"I am *really* going to get you, you
chubby, stubby mole!"
They made such a clatter the neighbors
rushed to their windows to see.

They thought it was Santa Claus and all
his reindeer.
Troll was getting closer. And
closer. And *closer*.
Mole jumped up onto the chimney. He
teetered. He tottered. And right down the
chimney he fell! Troll had a tight
grip on Mole's shoe. So he went
down right behind.

BUMP! THUMP! They landed in the
fireplace all covered with soot.
Mole stared at Troll.
Troll glared at Mole.
"*Star!*" he screamed.
"*Phooey on you!*" Mole screamed back.
"I am going home!"

He took what was left of his ornaments
and stomped out.
"Good," Troll said to himself.
"He doesn't know *anything* about
trimming a tree."
So Troll began to trim the tree alone.
He put up one bright red ornament. It
looked lonesome, so he took it down.
He put up colored lights. But they
didn't seem as cheerful as before. Even
the tinsel globs did not look so good.

Troll squeezed the tinsel into a big
ball and thought about Mole. He felt
glum.

He said to himself, "Troll, you are
a stinker. You are the worst troll I
know. Mole is your friend—even if he
throws berries. And you chased him away
with your big, loud voice. Trimming
the tree alone is no fun at all. And
now he will probably never do *anything*
with you ever, ever again. Oh, you are
such a stinker!"

"That is what *I* say!" said a voice
from the door. It was Mole.
Troll jumped up. But then Mole laughed.
Then they both laughed till they
shook all over.

"You are not really a stinker,"
said Mole. "You are my good friend,
and you can put anything you want on
the tree."
"It is *our* tree," said Troll,
"and you can put what *you* want on it,
too."

So they put everything in the world on their tree. They put gay colored lights and twinkling lights and a sheet for snow and some cotton for snow and cranberry strings and popcorn strings and gingerbread men and candy canes and gilded walnuts. They hung tinsel and colored balls and tiny toys and handmade floating balloons. They put some bearded dwarfs around the bottom. And they put a star *and* an angel on the very top.

1820615

At last the tree was done. There was
hardly any green showing.
They stood by the fire and watched the
lights.
"It is a beautiful tree," said
Troll.
"It is the best tree ever," said
Mole.

"It is really too nice to keep for
ourselves," said Troll. "Let's
take it outside for everyone to see!"
So Mole and Troll put the tree on the
toboggan. They pulled it out into the
square.

The neighbors all came. They thought it was
the prettiest tree they had ever seen.
At least it had the most things on it.

The tree twinkled in the soft winter
light. It put everyone in a joyful
Christmas mood. Some sang songs. Some
danced. Some just stood and watched.

Then they all clinked mugs of hot
chocolate and felt warm inside—
especially Mole and Troll.